THIS CHICKEN IS A T-REX!

WHITE STAR KIDS

THIS CHICKEN IS A T-REX!

The Great Big Book of Animal Evolution

Illustrations by
Román García Mora

Text by
Cristina M. Banfi, Cristina Peraboni and Rita Mabel Schiavo
Associazione Didattica Museale (ADM), Milan

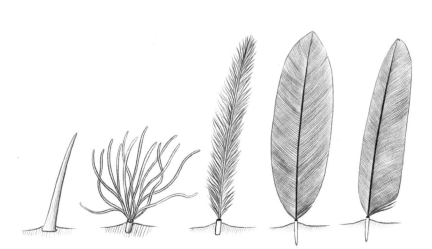

Almost as if they had come out of a fantasy novel, many animals from the past can appear scary, attractive or a little bit bizarre to our eyes. Even though they no longer exist today, we know about their existence and their appearance thanks to reconstructions made by paleontologists based on the findings of their fossil remains.

The science of fossils, or Paleontology, tells us that from the moment that life appeared on Earth up until today, there have been more than 250 million species of living beings. However, no species lives forever: at varying times, sooner or later, they all become **extinct**. Their disappearance is not necessarily caused by a violent event; very often, it is gradual and necessary to make way on the planet for new forms of life.

At any given time, there has always been a new species of living beings taking shape somewhere on Earth. Of course, they do not originate out of nothing, but come from **evolution**, the process that, starting from pre-existing forms, making changes at various speeds, generation after generation, until the descendants have very different characteristics from their ancestors. Evidence of evolution can be found in fossils, showing us how much or how little the organisms have changed over time.

If the environment in which the new species lives offers different ecological conditions that are beneficial to the survival of individuals, it is possible that many species will develop from that species, creating the phenomenon that scientists call **adaptive radiation**.

This has resulted in numerous varieties of living species developing on Earth, many of which can be found in the pages of this book. Some are curious and extravagant; others are extremely large or with bodies characterized by varied designs and colors, but all of them will be able to surprise you, showing off you their incredible transformations.

THE ORIGIN OF BIRDS

That chicken of a T-Rex

Could you ever confuse a T-Rex with a chicken? Certainly not! We have always thought of the first as a clever predator, the most feared of all the dinosaurs, while the chicken we see as a harmless animal and why not? It is even a little bit stupid. However, after long years of research and infinite debates, paleontologists have finally discovered that the closest living relative of the fierce T-Rex is the chicken. What is the proof? It seems to be a protein found in the fossils of the bones which is found today in birds and not found in reptiles. Therefore we have to look for the ancestors of birds among the Theropods, a group of carnivorous dinosaurs that, like their descendants, had bodies covered with feathers and which laid eggs.

200 MILLION YEARS AGO

A small group of Theropod dinosaurs, already equipped with feathers, began a progressive reduction in their body dimensions; they had the ability to glide.

100 MILLION YEARS AGO

The teeth of birds disappear, a characteristic that is more typically reptilian. From this time onwards, beaks of different shapes and sizes develop.

DEINONYCHUS

Its name means "terrible claw" because
this dinosaur had a sharp retractable
claw on both of its feet. But perhaps
even more curious were the feathers on its
body and on its front legs, which, even
if they did not allow for real flight,
helped it to make agile leaps onto the
back of prey.

TYRANNOSAURUS REX

Everyone knows the T-Rex, but perhaps not
everyone knows that recent paleontological studies say that it is more closely
related to a canary than to a lizard. It
belongs to the group of Theropods, carnivorous dinosaurs with highly developed
rear legs and front legs that were simple
stumps.

55 MILLION YEARS AGO

Birds develop the ability to fly by
batting their wings; at the same time,
their main prey, insects, begin a gradual reduction in size.

AND NOW, who can still say that all dinosaurs are extinct? Birds are flour-
ishing and they can tell us a lot about
their pre-historic "brothers". The research of paleontologists continues ...

A COMPARISON BETWEEN THE ARCHAEOPTERYX AND THE ROOSTER

The discovery in Solnhofen, Germany, of the fossil remains of a 150 million-year-old creature that featured many characteristics of birds alongside other typical dinosaurs created great surprise among scientists. It was called the Archaeopteryx, which means "ancient wing". Its long bony tail and mouth armed with small teeth made it seem, without any doubt, a small dinosaur, but the imprint of feathers on its front legs, similar to wings, were proof that it was also a bird. It was 1861 and very little was known yet about the relationships between these animals.

ARCHAEOPTERYX

The skeleton of the Archaeopteryx has some reptilian features including its tail, teeth, small skull and the claws on its hand. But it also has a furcula (wishbone), derived from the fusion of the two clavicles, and above all feathers of the type we find in all birds.

THE BONES OF BIRDS (and not those of the Archaeopteryx) are hollow to reduce the weight of the skeleton which must be able to rise up during flight. However, inside these bones, there is a set of structures that cross the cavity to form a frame giving strength to the bone.

FEATHERS AND PLUMAGE developed from a transformation of scales such as those found on reptiles. The first feathers were filamentous, then they grew in tufts and finally they developed into full feathers, whose strong, asymmetrical structure allowed for flight.

ROOSTER

ROOSTER

The rooster has a streamlined sternum whose shape allows for the attachment of the large, powerful chest muscles that allow for flight. No bird today has teeth, but they all have a beak whose shape depends on the type of food they consume.

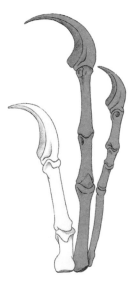

ARCHAEOPTERYX

VELOCIRAPTOR

A COMPARISON OF HANDS: the hand of the Archaeopteryx has characteristics that fall between that of a Velociraptor and that of a bird. You can see a gradual reduction in the number of fingers and the fusion that eventually led to the formation of wings in birds.

RATITES (flightless birds)

They're birds, but they don't fly!

This group is made up of the largest birds that have ever existed. The name Ratites derives from the Latin word *ratis*, or "raft", and refers to the flat shape of the sternum that is typical of flightless birds. In fact, such a large, massive body does not make them fit to fly gracefully in the air; instead, they are formidable runners, as their long legs and powerful thighs would imply. They are likely the descendants of ancient birds that could fly and that changed their mode of movement over time. Ratites today live only in the Southern Hemisphere.

AEPYORNIS

Madagascar's great bird-elephant disappeared in the 1700s. Its gigantic eggs, 3.3 ft (1 m) in diameter, have contributed to numerous legends, such as that of the fierce Roc's egg described in the book *One Thousand and One Nights*.

OSTRICH

Up to 8.85 ft (2.7 m) tall, the ostrich is the largest and fastest Ratite alive today, reaching speeds of up to 43.5 mph (70 km/h). Its eggs are also record-breaking as they weigh in at nearly 3.3 lb (1,5 kg).

DINORNIS

Known also by the name of Giant Moa, it may have been the tallest bird that ever lived at 11.8 ft (3.6 m). It lived in the forests of New Zealand and became extinct upon the arrival of man on the island.

Aepyornis

Ostrich

Apteryx

Rooster

Hummingbird

COMPARISON. A comparison of eggs made in real sizes of a selection of birds: the smallest eggs come from hummingbirds, they are only 0.4 in (1 cm) long and weigh less than 1 oz (0,25 g); the largest eggs come from ostriches, measuring 6.3 in (16 cm) with a weight of 3.3 lb (1.5 kg) and are the equivalent of 20 chicken eggs. And these are nothing when compared with the egg of the Aepyornis whose dimensions are record-breaking: 14.8 in (37.5 cm) long and weighing 26.5 lb (12 kg)!

THE EVOLUTION OF HORSES

Losing Its Toes

A bunch of horses gallop freely on the prairie, the beating of their hooves give the race its rhythm: it is difficult to imagine a close relationship between tapirs and rhinoceroses, all odd-toed ungulates, that is, animals with a reduced odd number of toes. When the climate became arid, the humid forests of the north gradually turned into grassland and some animals began to colonize this new environment. There were two problems to solve: how to eat the tough grasses of the steppes and how to escape enemies when there were no places to hide. From the small-sized Sifrhippus and Eohippus, the first as large as a cat and the second the size of a fox with a reduced number of hooves, a number of animals evolved which had specialized teeth and which were adapted to live on the tip of the only toe that rested on the ground!

PALEOTHERIUM

Its robust, long legs were located more towards the front of its body than the back and allowed it to move safely between the marshy areas of the forests.
It was 29.5 in (75 cm) tall and had a very long neck to be able to reach the leaves of the trees.

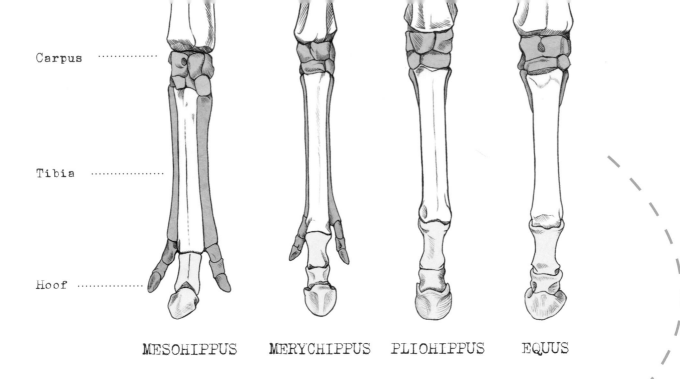

Carpus ············

Tibia ············

Hoof ············

MESOHIPPUS   MERYCHIPPUS   PLIOHIPPUS   EQUUS

COMPARISON. The hoof of modern horses is actually the nail of
the robust middle toe, supported by the bones that have been
integrated from the reduced number of phalanxes. What we call
the knee of a horse (carpus) is actually its wrist!

PRZEWALSKI HORSE

With its brush-cut mane and special
color, the "Mongolian pony" is the last
representative of wild horses that remains today and is similar to those
that were painted by prehistoric man.

MESOHIPPUS

The "mid-horse" galloped on the first
North American prairies, placing only
three of its four toes on the ground.
It ate fruit and twigs and no longer
possessed canine teeth.

SABER-TOOTHED FELINES

What a brilliant smile!

They are not the ancestors of the modern tigers or even less those of our common household friend: the Machairodontinae group became extinct, but not before it had terrorized the hominids that lived in the same era. It seems strange but, although their long canines were much stronger and more resistant than those of modern day large felines, their bite was a third less strong than that of a lion!
Their hunting method therefore had to be different, considering that in herds they could even go after the impressive Mammoth: they likely used their weight to knock the animal down and bite its throat or soft parts, penetrating deeply, and then let it die from bleeding.

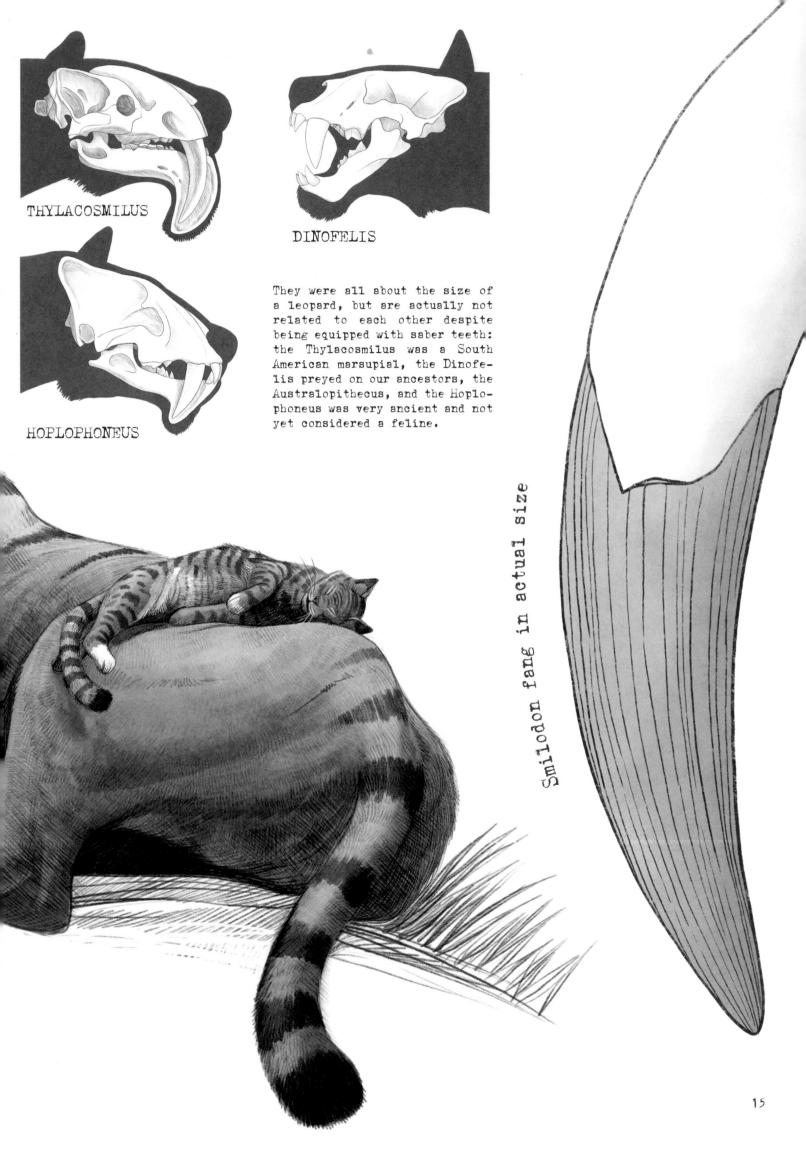

THYLACOSMILUS

DINOFELIS

HOPLOPHONEUS

They were all about the size of a leopard, but are actually not related to each other despite being equipped with saber teeth: the Thylacosmilus was a South American marsupial, the Dinofelis preyed on our ancestors, the Australopithecus, and the Hoplophoneus was very ancient and not yet considered a feline.

Smilodon fang in actual size

THE PROBOSCIDEA

A brief history of the very useful trunk!

The trunk of an elephant is, along with its tusks, the most evident of its characteristics. The trunk is derived from the fusion of the nose and upper lip and it moves using 40,000 muscles. It is highly versatile and is used by the elephant to breathe, smell, touch, grasp items and produce sounds. The history of the trunk begins in the distant past, about 60 million years ago in the forests of Africa. It evolved in order to assist the animals with their nutrition and was used for gathering vegetation. Over time, it has continued to grow in size along with the animal's body.

ELEPHANT

The African elephant is the largest land animal that lives today. With its trunk, an elephant can lift weights up to 772 lb (350 kg) and can sense the presence of water from several miles away.

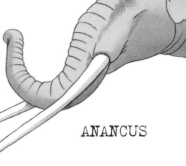

ANANCUS

MORITHERIUM

A long distant relative of modern elephants, the Moeritherium was more like a hippopotamus. It did not have a real trunk, but only a muscular upper lip that it used to harvest leaves.

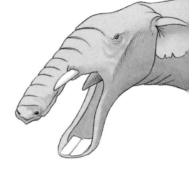

AMEBELODON

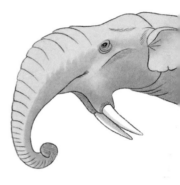

DEINOTHERIUM

COMPARISON. Paleontologists believe that more than 350 species of proboscideans have lived on Earth in the past: today, only elephants remain of this group of animals.

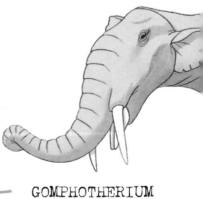

GOMPHOTHERIUM

MAMMOTH

A relative of the elephant, but not a direct ancestor, the Mammoth had a body covered with thick skin because it lived in the icy lands of the Northern Hemisphere during the Ice Age.

GIANT DRAGONFLIES

The super ancestors of the arthropods

There was a time when Earth's rulers were arthropods that, unlike today, reached truly incredible dimensions. Having been the first animals to colonize the emerged lands, they were differentiated in shape and size and occupied the entire planet. The atmosphere of the era was much more humid and it was richer in oxygen than the present one. This allowed many arthropods, which do not breathe with lungs but with the passage of air into the trachea, to become super-sized! The most common were giant insects and millipedes. As time progressed, the appearance of other animals, especially birds, gave way to their disappearance, favoring the emergence of new species that were much smaller-sized, similar to those we know today. One of the missing giants is the Arthropleura, a relative of the modern millipede, which lived between 340 and 280 million years ago. It is considered the largest terrestrial invertebrate of all time and is thought to have reached up to 8.2 ft (2.5 m) in length. Having never found parts of its mouth, paleontologists are still very uncertain about what it ate: was the Arthropleura a herbivore or a carnivore?

DRAGONFLY (CORDULEGASTER)

The dragonfly has a long abdomen and two pairs of very strong wings that allow it be agile and fast when in flight. It lives near ponds, rivers and puddles of water. Its larvae develop in water-based environments.

ARTHROPLEURA

PALAEODICTYOPTERA

These flying insects were 19.7 in (0.5 m) long and were found flying in Carboniferous forests feeding on the sap of trees.

MEGANEURA

It had a 29.5 in (75 cm) wingspan, making it as large as a seagull. The Meganeura was the largest arthropod capable of flying and, like modern dragonflies, was a predator.

LAND CROCODILES

Fangs and scales

On land, they seem indolent and sometimes remain almost motionless for hours, lying on their stomachs and short palmed limbs; they move forward slowly, weighed down by the scales that gave them the name of Loricata. It would seem to be impossible but some of their ancestors were able to run fast, rise up on two legs and jump like kangaroos! The long, robust tail that balanced out the movement is perfect in modern times for swimming. When compared to caymans and alligators, the characteristic grin is more evident in crocodiles as they have a long, narrow muzzle in which the lower canine teeth remain visible even when they close their mouths. They all catch their prey by mauling it, therefore their tapering teeth can break, but there is no need to worry: they can each be replaced up to four times!

TERRESTRISUCHUS

The small "land crocodile" reached only 19.7 in (50 cm) in length. With a head similar to that of a greyhound, a slim body and long limbs, especially the rear ones, it was a great runner.

ALLIGATOR

Mississippi's "El legarto", like all reptiles, grows for their entire life: at about fifty years old, it can reach over 16.4 ft (5 m) in length. When it moves forward slowly on land, it keeps its legs straight: but it cannot accelerate too much, otherwise it stumbles and crashes to the ground!

SILESAURUS

This relative of the dinosaurs was a herbivore and may have possessed a small hornlike beak to rip apart vegetation. It was lightweight and had very long rear legs that could assume a bipedal position.

ALLIGATOR   DEINOSUCHUS

COMPARISON. The "terrible crocodile" was actually a giant alligator that could reach up to 46 ft (14 m) in length, that is, triple that of its current descendant. With its large jaws, it preyed on large dinosaurs and other animals that drank in North American rivers. Its bite was more powerful than that of a T-Rex.

A COLLECTION OF STRANGE CROCODILES

Defined as "living fossils" because they have maintained the same characteristics for thousands of years, it was not easy for paleontologists to recognize a group of unusual fossils as their ancestors. There were those that were not able to swim, those that had maple-leaf shaped teeth and ate only vegetation like the Simosuchus, and those that barely reached 3.3 ft (1 m) in length.

LAGANOSUCHUS

The "pancake crocodile" was a green lizard that was 16.4 ft (5 m) in length, of which 3.3 ft (1 m) was its flat head. It stayed motionless in the low waters of the Sahara waiting in ambush for its prey.

ANATOSUCHUS

A long flat muzzle was characteristic of the "crocodile duck". The smallest representative of this group, it grew to only 2.3 ft (70 cm) in length and caught small prey in the water.

KAPROSUCHUS

Huge teeth that were similar to fangs gave it the name of "crocodile boar". Its muzzle included a kind of shield at the end. From the fossils of its skull, it is assumed to have had a total length of 19.7 ft (6 m).

SIMOSUCHUS

Madagascar, known for its population of large dinosaurs and carnivorous crocodiles, was also home to this small, bizarre "pugnosed crocodile" that moved around on its robust limbs to look for leaves, protected by hornlike scales on its head, back, tail and legs.

23

GIANT WOMBATS

In the realm of marsupials, but not only ...

Marsupials are strange mammals: they carry their newborns in a "pouch" until they are big enough to look after themselves. It may seem to be an uncomfortable system, but it obviously has some advantages as the entire continent of Australia is almost exclusively inhabited by this group of mammals. Many marsupials, such as the well-known kangaroos, but also others that are lesser known such as the wombat, had much larger ancestors than the modern versions of these species.

WOMBAT

The wombat is a herbivorous marsupial about the size of a large dog and looks like a bear cub. It can be friendly with mankind, but if it is provoked, it will defend itself by biting.

DIPROTODON

The ancestors of the modern wombats could reach the size of rhinoceroses, but this did not prevent them from being exterminated by the ancient inhabitants of Australia and therefore becoming extinct.

HUNTING A PROCOPTODON

Even kangaroos had their giants: the Procoptodon grazed on grass and was certainly able to make long jumps to escape predators, but suffered the same fate as the Diprotodon and was made extinct at the hands of the ancient Aborigines.

DIPROTODON

WOMBAT

A COMPARISON between the skulls of a Diprotodon and a modern wombat. The giant Diprotodon's tremendous set of teeth, suitable for chewing the vegetation that it fed on, but also for defending itself from predators, are immediately noticeable.

AUSTRALIAN MEGAFAUNA

Throughout the passage of the ages, the immense Australian continent has been inhabited by truly strange animals. Separated from other lands since ancient times, Australia allowed marsupials to evolve into many different forms which resemble the insectivores, rodents, herbivores and carnivores that live on other continents. This phenomenon is referred to as "evolutionary convergence" and occurs when species belonging to different groups, such as a predatory marsupial and a feline, develop similar forms and lifestyle habits. But in Australia, there are, and there were in past times, animals even more strange than marsupials: giant birds and mammals that laid eggs!

PALORCHESTES

This strange marsupial from the past seems to have been a cross between a bear and a tapir: it had powerful claws that would have made a grizzly bear envious and a shortened trunk. Little is known about the habits of the Palorchestes which were probably similar to those of the current tapirs.

PROCOPTODON

This was the giant of the kangaroos: extinct in modern times, it was about 9.8 ft (3 m) in length, had very long legs with a single toe containing a claw and, like modern kangaroos, grazed on low-lying vegetation. Thanks to its height, by standing up on its back legs, it could see danger from far away.

DROMORNIS

9.8 ft (3 m) tall and as heavy as six men, this bird ran on powerful legs and did not have many enemies. It does not however seem to have been a predator, but it fed on fruits and nuts that it could easily break apart with its strange, powerful beak.

ZAGLOSSUS HACKETTI

This extinct echidna was not very different from the ones still living in Australia today, it was just a little bigger. Echidnas are monotremes, mammals that lay eggs, and seem to have been somewhat of a cross between a porcupine and an ant eater: like the latter, they fed on ants and termites.

THYLACOLEO

The name of this predator means "lion marsupial" and it was surely the terror of wombats and giant kangaroos in its time. It is a good example of "evolutionary convergence": a marsupial with the teeth of a carnivore, powerful muscles, and claws suitable for grasping its prey, just like a real lion!

GIANT SLOTHS

The giant ancestor of the slowest animal in the world.

Growing to be gigantic in size is a good way to stay safe from enemies. If we add having claws that were 1 ft (30 cm) long, there would be no predator that we would be afraid of ... or would there? The sad story of the giant sloths shows us that there is no real defense against intelligence. It was actually a small predator that put an end to their existence: man! Numerous bones from these enormous, peaceful animals have been found in the caves of primitive men.

MEGATHERIUM

The scientific name means "great beast" and it is certainly appropriate: reaching up to 19.7 ft (6 m) tall and weighing more than an elephant, this ancestor of modern-day sloths certainly had no need to climb trees to reach the leaves that it fed on!

MODERN SLOTH

Sloths are typically arboreal, that is, they spend most of their lives in trees, using their curved claws to cling to branches.

In the detailed view of a finger, the size of the claw can be seen

COMPARISON of the size of the African elephant with that of the Megatherium.

ELEPHANT   MEGATHERIUM

GIANT ARMADILLOS

Many different models of live "tanks"

There are many ways for animals to defend themselves from predators including being fast enough to escape, or agile enough to climb to the top of trees, or knowing how to fly ... but what can an animal that does not have all these capabilities do? The ancestors of armadillos chose a slower but safer road: they became large and armored!
If you are as large as an off-road vehicle, there are very few predators that can make you afraid. If you also have armor, impenetrable to fangs and claws, you can graze in peace without paying too much attention to what's happening around you.

GLYPTODON

The Glyptodon, the largest of the giant armadillos, was
8.2 ft (2.5 m) long and had a long tail that was shaken
to the right and left for defense.

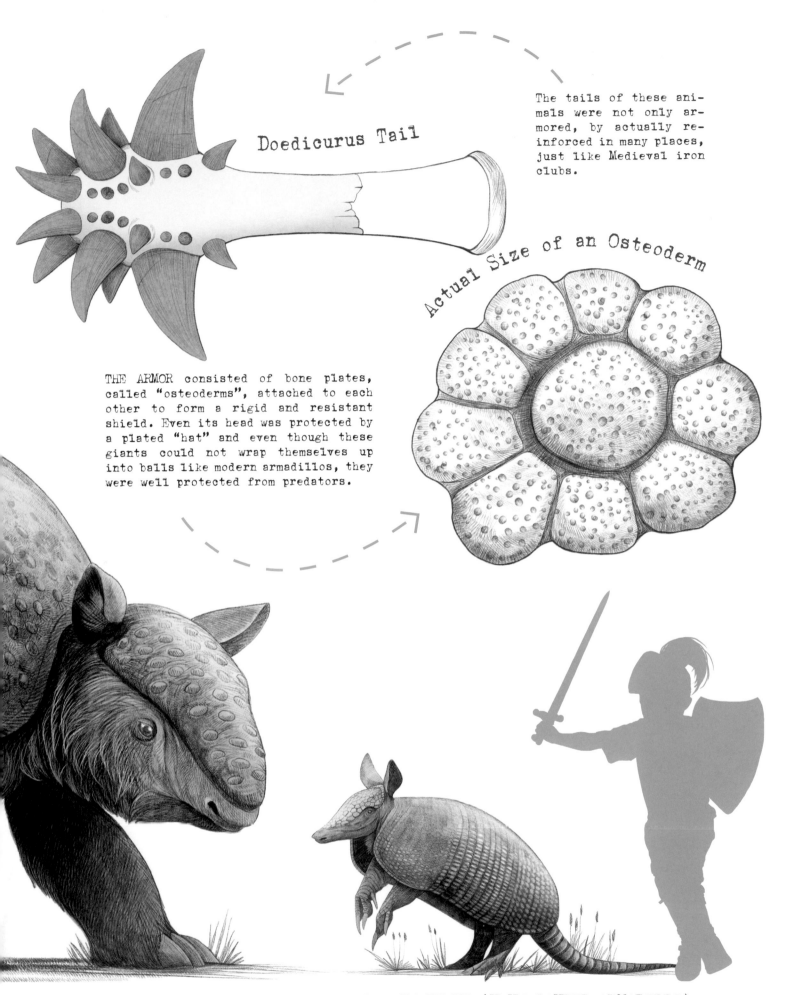

Doedicurus Tail

The tails of these animals were not only armored, by actually reinforced in many places, just like Medieval iron clubs.

Actual Size of an Osteoderm

THE ARMOR consisted of bone plates, called "osteoderms", attached to each other to form a rigid and resistant shield. Even its head was protected by a plated "hat" and even though these giants could not wrap themselves up into balls like modern armadillos, they were well protected from predators.

DASYPUS NOVEMCINCTUS (NINE-BANDED ARMADILLO)

The common armadillo is the largest among the species that are found today. It is more agile than its ancestors and can roll up into a ball or dig a hole quickly to hide underground in order to defend itself.

A WOLF IN SHEEP'S CLOTHING

Or a sheep in wolf's clothing?

What is the connection between a wolf and a sheep? Simple: the sheep is one of the favorite prey of the wolf. It is difficult to imagine that the ancestors of sheep were closely related to giant wolves. This does not refer to the ancestors of the wolves, but instead to carnivorous animals with a similar appearance and the same high level of hunger. What did they have in common? Some skeletal features, and particularly their limbs which ended in hooves. They each had even-toed ungulates as ancestors, that is, animals that placed an even number of toes on the ground, like modern sheep. Included in this group is the Andrewsarchus skull. Its discovery was initially considered to be the largest carnivore that ever existed, but it was later downsized when compared to Entelodonts which were similar to wild boars and as large as rhinoceroses though they had brains as small as a golf ball.

SHEEP

Covered with thick wool, it places its limbs on the ground with hooves containing the two toes which remain.

ANDREWSARCHUS

With a body similar to that of an imposing hyena and limbs which included small hooves, it had a thick mane to defend itself from any attacks.

MESONYX

This fast, long-legged runner had small hooves and a
skull typical of carnivores
with a powerful bite, but
it was one of the ancestors
of dolphins!

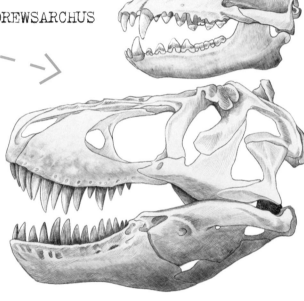

ANDREWSARCHUS

COMPARISON. Powerful teeth, all tapered in
the large reptile and of different shapes
in the mammal, allowed these opportunists
to tear large herbivores to pieces or to
eat dead animals. While the 32.7 in (83
cm) skull of the mammal was dispro-
portionate in relation to the body,
in the 39.3 ft (12 m) length of
the dinosaur, the robust neck
was able to support the 3.9
ft (1.20 m) long skull which
weighed 1.1 tons (1 tonne).

T-REX

MASTIFF

THE EVOLUTION OF WHALES

The giants of the sea

Recent studies seem to confirm the hypothesis that whales and hippopotamuses descend from a common ancestor. This creature lived near the water and from it, animals with increasingly-hydrodynamic bodies and fins suitable for swimming would evolve. Baleen whales and blue whales are Cetaceans, from the Greek word meaning "sea monsters", a definition given to them due to their giant size. They feed on small fish and shrimp known as Krill which they eat in large quantities by sucking water into their mouth and filtering out the fish through a baleen, a huge comb-like structure in their mouths.

DORUDON

It could reach up to 16.4 ft (5 m) in length and this predator caught fish and molluscs to eat. It was able to swim thanks to four fins and a tail similar to that of modern whales.

PAKICETUS

Considered the earliest ancestor of whales, this carnivore was the size of a wolf and lived alongside water sources in present day Pakistan, where it caught its prey on land.

BALAENOPTERA

Four finger-like bones extended inside the fins of some animals and allowed the larger ones to "fly" in the water. At 108.2 ft (33 m) long and weighing 172 tonnes (190 tons), the blue whale can reach up to 30 mph (50 km/h).

RODHOCETUS

At 8.2 ft (2.5 m) in length, it lived an amphibious lifestyle, able to swim easily on the surface of the water with its long limbs, but having difficulty when walking on land because it weighed more than 1100 lb (500 kg).

PREHISTORIC SHARKS

The most fearsome predators of the sea from the past ... and the present

Sharks are very ancient creatures: the first species appeared in saltwater seas and freshwater lakes on Earth almost 200 million years before the dinosaurs. Among the most ancient sharks, there were species with bizarre shapes, some small and others gigantic, but overall, the "basic model" remained practically unchanged. Modern sharks are not very different from those that lived millions of years ago. Like their ancestors, they are perfect predators, fast, powerful and armed with teeth that are not seen in any other species.

HELICOPRION

The most notable feature of this shark is its row of teeth that were arranged to form a kind of circular saw. This structure is still a mystery to scholars who have not been able to find a convincing hypothesis about its possible function.

WHITE SHARK

This shark is the most fearsome member of the modern day sea predators. It can reach up to 19.7 ft (6 m) in length and its large triangular teeth have sharp, sawed-off edges that do not allow prey of any size to get away.

MEGALODON

WHITE SHARK

A COMPARISON of the size of the Megalodon
with the modern-day white shark. Based on
the fossils of jawbones that have been
found, the Megalodon could reach a length
of up to 59 ft (18 m).

Megalodon and white shark teeth

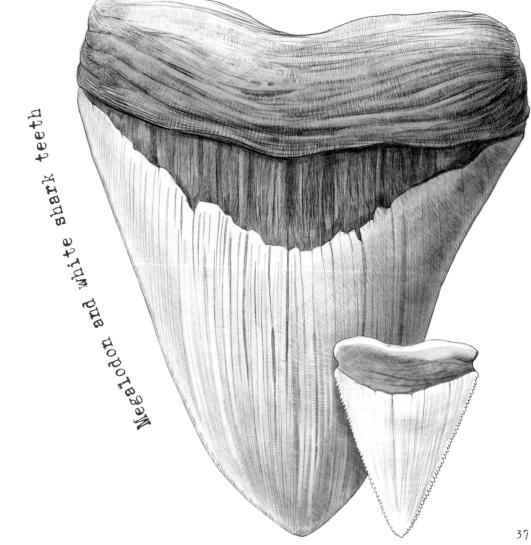

A STRANGE COLLECTION OF RELATIVES!

Before vertebrates even "landed" on the mainland, fish had hundreds of millions of years to evolve. The mechanisms of evolution often led to species that became extinct without leaving descendants and we only know of them thanks to a few fossil fragments. This is the case for many species of fish, as old as they are strange, for which paleontologists are only able to make assumptions about how they lived, fed, or reproduced.

STETHACANTHUS

This little shark, about 27.5 in (70 cm) long, had a strange dorsal fin shaped like an anvil whose function remains a mystery: no other sharks are known to have had a similar structure!

PAREXUS

Older than the first sharks, the class
of acanthodian fish to which the Par-
exus belonged, had rows of spines or
thorns along their body and fins. For
this reason, they are often called
"spiny sharks".

ORTHACANTHUS

This shark was about 9.8 ft (3 m) long
and lived in freshwater areas about
400 million years ago. It had a long
dorsal fin and a flexible body that
made it look like a giant eel.

39

Associazione Didattica Museale was founded in 1994 and has been operating in the field of education for more than 20 years. It manages the Educational Services of important museums including the Museums of Natural History in Milan, Genoa, Novara and Trieste. It also organizes the didactic program on natural oases and public and private parks. Contributors to this volume include Cristina M. Banfi, Cristina Peraboni and Rita Mabel Schiavo.

Attracted since childhood by both art and science, **Román García Mora** graduated in biology. After his studies, he decided to unite the two fields that fascinated him and specialized in scientific illustration, devoting himself in particular to paleontological reconstruction, above all of dinosaurs. Román has received several international awards in this field. He has worked for several scientific journals such as "pm bilde quo" and collaborates with various publishers and illustrated scientific publications, along with researchers from several spanish institutions. In the past years, he has realized several books for White Star Kids, with great enthusiasm and creativity.

WHITE STAR KIDS

White Star Kids® is a registered trademark property of White Star s.r.l.

© 2017 White Star s.r.l.
Piazzale Luigi Cadorna, 6 - 20123 Milan, Italy
www.whitestar.it

Translation: TperTradurre S.r.l.

ISBN 978-88-544-1197-5
1 2 3 4 5 6   21 20 19 18 17

Printed in China